How's the Weather?

Today Is Windy

by Martha E. H. Rustad

Consulting Editor: Gail Saunders-Smith, PhD

Consultant: J. Kevin Lavin, Executive Director
National Weather Association, Charlottesville, Virginia

Capstone
press
Mankato, Minnesota

Pebble Plus is published by Capstone Press,
151 Good Counsel Drive, P.O. Box 669, Mankato, Minnesota 56002.
www.capstonepress.com

1 2 3 4 5 6 11 10 09 08 07 06

Library of Congress Cataloging-in-Publication Data
Rustad, Martha E. H. (Martha Elizabeth Hillman), 1975–
    Today is windy / by Martha E. H. Rustad.
    p. cm.—(Pebble plus. How's the weather?)
    Summary: "Simple text and photographs present weather information, clothing choices, and activities
for a windy day"—Provided by publisher.
    Includes bibliographical references and index.
    ISBN-13: 978-0-7368-5347-7 (hardcover)
    ISBN-10: 0-7368-5347-2 (hardcover)
    1. Winds—Juvenile literature. 2. Weather protection—Equipment and supplies—Juvenile literature.
I. Title. II. Series.
QC931.4.R87 2006
551.51'8—dc22   200502079

Editorial Credits
Sarah L. Schuette, editor; Ted Williams, designer; Jo Miller, photo researcher; Scott Thoms, photo editor

Photo Credits
Capstone Press/Karon Dubke, cover (child), 1, 11, 13, 20–21
Corbis/Eric and David Hosking, 6–7; Neil Rabinowitz, 17; zefa/J. Jamsen, cover; zefa/Roy Morsch, 14–15
Getty Images Inc./Photographer's Choice/Chris Hackett, 21 (inset); Photonica/Mark Donet, 4–5;
    Stone/John Lawrence, 9
Grant Heilman Photography, 19

The author dedicates this book to her son, Leif Anton Rustad.

Note to Parents and Teachers

The How's the Weather? set supports national science standards related to climate
and weather. This book describes and illustrates a windy day. The images support
early readers in understanding the text. The repetition of words and phrases helps early
readers learn new words. This book also introduces early readers to subject-specific
vocabulary words, which are defined in the Glossary section. Early readers may need
assistance to read some words and to use the Table of Contents, Glossary, Read More,
Internet Sites, and Index sections of the book.

Table of Contents

A Windy Day

Today the weather is windy.

The air blows and swirls.

The wind whistles
through the trees.
Leaves fall slowly
to the ground.

Flags flap above the buildings.

Clouds move with the wind.

9

What I Wear

I wear a jacket

to stay warm

on a cool windy day.

I wear a hat.

It keeps the wind

from blowing my hair.

What We Do

We fly kites.

They float high in the sky.

We watch sailboats.

A gust of wind pushes them

across the water.

We blow bubbles.
The gentle breeze
carries them away.

19

How's the Weather?

Today is windy.

What will the weather

be like tomorrow?

Glossary

air—the gasses around the earth; we need air to breathe; wind is moving air.

breeze—a light wind

cloud—a white or gray mass of water droplets and dust in the air; raindrops form in certain kinds of clouds.

gust—a sudden, strong blast of wind

weather—the condition outdoors at a certain time and place; weather can be cold, hot, calm, windy, rainy, dry, sunny, or cloudy.

Read More

Nelson, Robin. *Windy*. First Step Nonfiction. Minneapolis: Lerner, 2005.

Sherman, Josepha. *Gusts and Gales: A Book About Wind.* Amazing Science. Minneapolis: Picture Window Books, 2004.

Williams, Judith. *Why Is It Windy?* I Like Weather! Berkeley Heights, N.J. : Enslow, 2005.

Internet Sites

FactHound offers a safe, fun way to find Internet sites related to this book. All of the sites on FactHound have been researched by our staff.

Here's how:

1. Visit *www.facthound.com*

2. Type in this special code **0736853472** for age-appropriate sites. Or enter a search word related to this book for a more general search.

3. Click on the **Fetch It** button.

FactHound will fetch the best sites for you!

Index

Word Count: 96
Grade: 1
Early-Intervention Level: 13